ADMINISTRATIVE PROCEDURES AND MANAGEMENT

MARGARITA SAIDALI and
JAM FERDINAND SAIDALI

PARTRIDGE

Copyright © 2019 by Margarita Saidali and Jam Ferdinand Saidali.

ISBN:	Softcover	978-1-5437-5275-5
	eBook	978-1-5437-5276-2

All rights reserved. No part of this book may be used or reproduced by any means, graphic, electronic, or mechanical, including photocopying, recording, taping or by any information storage retrieval system without the written permission of the author except in the case of brief quotations embodied in critical articles and reviews.

Because of the dynamic nature of the Internet, any web addresses or links contained in this book may have changed since publication and may no longer be valid. The views expressed in this work are solely those of the author and do not necessarily reflect the views of the publisher, and the publisher hereby disclaims any responsibility for them.

Print information available on the last page.

To order additional copies of this book, contact
Toll Free 800 101 2657 (Singapore)
Toll Free 1 800 81 7340 (Malaysia)
orders.singapore@partridgepublishing.com

www.partridgepublishing.com/singapore

CONTENTS

Module 1	Overview of an Office Administration	1
Module 2	The Nature of Office Management	8
Module 3	The Office Organizational Structure	17
Module 4	Administrative Office Procedures	26
Module 5	Office Space Planning & Ergonomics	34
Module 6	Dealing with Visitors	46
Module 7	Correspondence	53
Module 8	Records Management System	61
Module 9	Travel Arrangements	78
Module 10	Handling Meetings	82
Module 11	Managing for Personal Effectiveness	91

MODULE 1
OVERVIEW OF AN OFFICE ADMINISTRATION

The Bureau of Labor Statistics of U.S. Department of Labor which was published in 2017, reflects the employment projections of office management career for 2014-2024 decade. The profile describes that both the occupations for Customer Service Representatives and Receptionists will be doing good and continue to grow up to 10%. Likewise, the positions of Secretaries, Administrative Assistants and General Office Clerks job which is also projected to grow up to 3%. More demands is for medical assistants with a view of increasing up to 23% percent.

The work of an office administrator is vital to an organization due to the duties and responsibilities entrusted to them. Specialized training and right attitude is required for them to deal with a diverse workforce, and to work effectively and efficiently.

A student currently studying administrative office course or who have left college can have the opportunity to work as general office staff. He will gain experience and will expose him to an extensive range of roles in the administrative office. If he shows good initiative and is able to work under pressure when given a task, he will survive and later a permanent work status can be a reward for him.

Employer Expectations

Employer hired employee with an expectation that he has a set of qualities, attributes, and skills that can contribute to the success of the organization. The technical skills required depends on the job position, however the personal and professional qualities may likewise be similar for all employers.

1. Open-mindedness. An open-minded person has the willingness to learn new things; in other word he is teachable. He listens very well, welcome new ideas, had a cooperative attitude and show a degree of flexibility in work. Being open-minded also means being tolerant, fair-minded and receptive.
2. Flexibility. An employee who has a flexible mindset can do different tasks even outside his job descriptions. He is more than willing to take responsibilities whatever is necessary to meet the goal of the company.
3. Commitment. When employee is committed to his work he is like an ambassador for his company, both inside and outside of office. The boss will prefers someone who is always willing, supportive and productive.
4. Reliability and Accountability. Reliability and accountability are essential traits to employee performance. Reliability consists of the extent to which an individual may be counted on to do what is expected of him.
5. Proactive. Employer expects his new employee to be proactive. Proactive employee thinks and acts in advance before the employer ask to do something and will usually require less instruction.

Employers' Responsibilities

Employer has the responsibility to his employee once he was hired. These are the main ones:

1. A prepared job description is already set tailored to the position and the employee. The vision, goals and objectives of the company must be explained clearly to the new employee.
2. Employers must see to it that the employee has a comfortable place to work with.
3. Employers must pay his employee according to the salary and benefits they agreed to, including other monetary benefits such as vacation leave, holidays and other mandatory paid leaves.
4. A safe working condition is to be taken care of by the employer. An inspection of the workplace should be done annually.
5. Employer must give the employee written notice of concern regarding his employment.
6. Employer must treat his employee with respect.

The Employees' Responsibilities

The responsibility works two ways, employee have also responsibility to his employer. These are the main responsibilities of employees:

1. Obedience. Obeying rules and policies of the company;
2. Dealing honestly with the employer, not lying or stealing from the employer.
3. Work with reasonable care and skill at the job assigned during the time required. In other words, giving full value of the time for which the employee is being paid.

4. Not to disclose confidential employer information to others.
5. Not to disclose any possible conflict of interest, such as work for a competitor or a relationship that could compromise the employer.
6. To care for the employer's property, equipment, and facilities.
7. To be loyal

The Office

An office is generally a room or other area where administrative work is done, but may also denote a position within an organization with specific duties, such as the president, manager, supervisor, secretary and the staff.

People is use to travel from home to office to work, this is done for almost centuries. Today, office has changed from physical spaces to respond to cultural, technological and social forces. Changes in technology also influenced the office. Now digital maturity seems a signal to the end of the office, with online connectivity, where people could potentially work from home. The office of the future may be as familiar as home, but only time will tell.

Office Management

Administrative Office management is the way of dealing with the things in the office in an efficient way. Running the company by doing administrative duties is a form of office management.

Within small organizations, the responsibilities of office management may fall entirely on one individual, such as the entrepreneur or office manager. Within larger organizations, office management is usually a team effort overseen by the office manager and facilitated by receptionists, administrative assistants and filing clerks. Office management entails a high volume of coordination with staff, management, vendors and clients to accomplish tasks that are crucial to the overall operations of the office.

Administrative office management is generally considered to be within the middle-management level of the organizational hierarchy. In some organizations, especially in larger ones, administrative office management typically is an important component of the functional areas such as administrative services area.

LEARNING ASSESSMENT   SCORE _____

| NAME_____ YEAR/SECTION_____ DATE_____ |

I. Write your answer to questions given below.

1. List down the 5 responsibilities of the employer to his employee.

2. Give the modern definition of 'an office'.

3. List down the 7 responsibilities of the employee to his employer.

4. Can you tell the similarity and the differences in the tasks of an administrative assistant to the secretary?

5. Draw a pyramid and put three horizontal lines inside. Identify each line according to the levels of management. From the 3 level in the pyramid where is the position of the administrative officer.

6. Identify the office and administrative occupations whose job outlook projections are declining.

7. What are the reasons of the decline of those you identified above?

MODULE 2

THE NATURE OF OFFICE MANAGEMENT

Office management is important to business organization since its nature is to guide, direct, coordinate and control all services offered by the business. Office managers supervise administrative staff and are responsible for their jobs to be done efficiently. So, it is the function of office management to plan, organize, to staff, lead, control and coordinate the activities of the business to achieve its objectives.

To understand office management, it is imperative that we break it down into five managerial functions.

Functions of Office Management

1. **Planning** is the first step towards other functions of the office. It is choosing future courses of action from among other alternatives.
2. **Organizing** is included in the planning stage of the executive management with the support of office management. This include the designing of structure of roles of people in the organization, the arrangement of jobs to people in groups, the duties and functions to be defined to determine authority relationship so that the office functions well.

3. **Staffing** involves the selection, recruitment, compensation, promotion, training and development; and retirement of personnel which process has to be manned and managed by the office management
4. **Leading** is the process of guiding and supervising the subordinates to the various activities in the office so that they will contribute to organization and group goals.
5. **Controlling** is basis to the office management function of checking current performance against pre-determined office standards of the job. Job performance of the staff has to be measured to make sure that the goals of the office are attained.
6. **Coordination** will be successful if there is harmony among individual efforts toward the attainment of group goals. It is a process of teamwork, where in a workplace group there is a common goals and ownership of shared responsibility in achieving the goal.

The Role of Office Manager

An Office manager makes certain that the office will run efficiently on its day-to-day operation. His responsibilities include: organizing, calling, and conducting meetings; supervising and monitoring the administrative work of the staff; handling correspondence; records keeping for safety; deals with complaints and quarries; organize seminars and events; arrange hotel accommodations and transportation; supervise office layouts; order furniture and other office supplies; maintain office procedures and other administrative tasks; attend meetings with executive management; assist in selecting, hiring, orienting new hires. On the other hand the role of the office manager will always depend on the size and structure of the organization.

Office Manager's Skills

An Office manager is a multi-tasking person, supervising, and handling every detailed operation which can involve many different staff members. It is essential that an office manager has a strong leadership skills, management and operational skills. The following skills are consider essential: interpersonal skills; problem assessment and solving skills; leadership abilities; oral and written communication skills; knowledge to handle several office concerns without compromising effectiveness and efficiency; time management; preparation of reports, legal documents, and letters; detailed oriented; records management; inventory management and planning; spreadsheet preparation; PowerPoint; even budget preparation and expense reduction.

> **Management Thoughts:**
> *Self-knowledge is the beginning of self-improvement.*

Classroom Activity

The following are situational problems that need to be addressed. The problems presented showed that there are specific risks and threat that the management as well as the office manager may face in the workplace or outside the office but still connected to the work.

This is a valuable skill for you to develop not only for the Case Studies, but also for your future Consulting career. Being able to identify the key issues and structure your response to a business problem well is important for the Case Studies.

The students and the teacher need to address these problems and create useful learning tools for the discussion of the class.

THINGS TO THINK

The call comes in.

> Someone's being stalked;
> Two employees get into a shoving match;
> A woman flees a violently abusive mate;
> A sometimes disoriented employee keeps showing up at coworkers' homes;
> A supervisor's constant abuse infuriates a subordinate;
> An employee in a fit of rage destroys company property;
> A fired employee makes a direct threat.

These are just a few examples of the types of incidents that can happen in the workplace.

How each office manager responds to these reports will differ, not only among different organizations, but sometimes within the same organization, depending upon the circumstances of each situation. Even in organizations with highly structured, well-thought-out procedures in place, the handling will have to depend on:

- The nature of the incident;
- The circumstances surrounding the incident;
- Who is available to respond;
- Who has the skills to deal with the particular situation.

Question:

1. What is the most effective way to handle these situations?
   1.1 take a team approach, rather than having one manager, function or
   1.2 Office handles situations alone.

Follow up questions:

1. Do we agree with the approach presented to by the class?
2. If not, why wouldn't that approach work for?
3. What other approaches would work for?
4. Do the class have adequate resources to handle such a situation?

Case Study

"Sexual Assault"

A female employee came into the office of the Director of Security and reported that a male coworker had sexually assaulted her. The female employee explained that while the two employees were leaving a work area, the male coworker turned off the lights, reached both arms around her and grabbed her breasts. The male coworker was interviewed and denied intentionally touching her breasts. He did admit he might have brushed against her breast with his elbow.

Both employees indicated that they had been working together for approximately one year. They also both admitted that they had a close working and personal relationship on and off the job. They indicated that they had lunch together on a daily basis and had met outside the workplace at a cocktail lounge for drinks. They also admitted that they had hugged and kissed each other in the past.

There was insufficient evidence to prove sexual assault and the matter was turned over to the Equal Employment Opportunity (EEO) and Sexual Harassment personnel in the Human Resources Office for further determination.

1. The EEO Manager wanted the case turned over to their office; however, it was important to treat the incident as a criminal matter. A copy of the investigation was sent to

them after the investigation was completed. It is much more difficult to bring criminal charges of sexual assault/harassment if the investigation is not conducted by a trained criminal investigator.
2. Although 50% of marriages start in the workplace, companies should discourage employees from having a personal relationship at work.

LEARNING ASSESSMENT   SCORE _____

NAME_____ YEAR/SECTION_____DATE_____

I. **Identification.**

_____ 1. Manager has knowledge and proficiency in activities involving methods, processes, and procedures. Thus, it involves working with tools and specific techniques.

_____ 2. Is the ability to solve problems in ways that will benefit the enterprise. To be effective, particularly at upper organizational levels, managers must be able to do more than see a problem.

_____ 3. Manager has the ability to work with people; it is cooperative effort; it is teamwork; it is the creation of an environment in which people feel secure and free to express their opinions.

_____ 4. Manager has the ability to serve the "big picture". It is also about recognizing significant elements in a situation, and to understand the relationships among the elements.

_____ 5. He was charged with the responsibility of taking actions that will make it possible for individuals to make their best contributions to group objectives.

_____ 6. The level of management that spend more time on planning and organizing.

_____ 7. Is the essence of manager-ship for achieving harmony among individual efforts toward the accomplishment of group goal.

_____ 8-10. There are three manager's objectives, name them.

_____ 11. Conduct the affairs of business, to have work under control and to provide direction, to guide other employees, to administer and organize work processes and systems, and to handle problems.

_____ 12. First line supervisors' function deals much on this.

II. True or False

_____ 13. Managers lead effectively and efficiently if resources never become production.

_____ 14. Top management focus on design function.

_____ 15. Supervisors usually focus more on work productivity.

_____ 16. Management functions and skills vary at various management levels.

17. Not all middle management carry out managerial functions.

18. Functions of planning and organizing are a function of the top management.

19. Efficiency is the achievement of objectives while effectiveness is the achievement of it with the least amount of resources.

III. Give a short note. 10 points each.

1. Explain why middle-management level must have greater conceptual skills than supervisory level; while a supervisor must have greater technical and interpersonal skills than top management.

2. Manager has to perform the five functions of management. If you're the manager explain briefly how you will perform those functions.

3. Explain the management objectives the way you understand it.

MODULE 3

THE OFFICE ORGANIZATIONAL STRUCTURE

A formal outline of a company's structure makes it easier to add new positions in the company, as well as providing a flexible and ready means for growth.

The Organizational Structure

Small to medium sized companies have a structure like the one shown in the chart. The people who work for the company are divided into teams or working groups.

In a huge or big sized companies, the structure is more complex, it has several levels of positions which is called hierarchical levels. The best examples are San Miguel Corporation, Ayala Group of Companies, and etc., as well as the local and national governments.

Organizational structures can have the following types: (1) flat organizational structure; and (2) tall organizational structure. Flat organization structure is easy to handle, it is not expensive since the office has few people to compensate. This flat organizational structure is common on small businesses like entrepreneurial business and partnership. The employees report directly to the owner-manager.

The characteristics of flat organizational structure:

1. There are relatively few layers of management.
2. In a flat structure, front-line employees are empowered to make a range of decisions on their own.
3. Communication flows from the top-level management down to employees and back to top management.

Large corporations use the tall organizational structure. There are numerous layers of management in a tall organizational structure. The decision-making powers all rest with the top management. The decision making and authority are all centralized and all the strategic functions are segregated into departments. Information flows are generally one-way in a tall structure — from the top down.

The authority in a large organization consists of three levels.

1. **Top Management** (board of directors, chairman and managing director or stockholders in a closed corporation)
2. **Middle Manager** (administrative, production, financial, marketing and purchase managers)
3. **Supervisors**. Each of these supervisors fulfills a task for which he or she has been trained.

Positions, Tasks, and Responsibilities

The common positions, tasks and responsibilities found in most of the offices are the following:

1. Office Manager.

    1. Manage employment and human resources through developing employment policies and requirements.
    2. Establish rules for authority delegation.
    3. Act as the leader of office employees.
    4. Provide and maintain employee training and development programs.
    5. Determine office tasks and assign duties to employees.
    6. Develop performance criteria.
    7. Establish inter- and intra-office communications and monitor interpersonal interactions.
    8. Develop employee development and motivation programs.
    9. Approve and lead various meetings and conferences.
    10. Report senior management on office performance and issues.

2. Finance Manager.

    1. Formulate budget estimates in support of business objectives.
    2. Develop plans for allocating financial resources.
    3. Provide cash flow control and audit.
    4. Plan and control fund inflows and outflows.
    5. Manage office procurement and supply.
    6. Conduct financial analysis and examine trends.
    7. Review and interpret accounting and financial management policies.
    8. Review and verify accounts documentation.

9. Conduct financial audits and checks.
10. Make recommendations regarding cost saving policies.

3. Administrative Assistant.

    1. Administer office accessories supply.
    2. Report Office Manager on employee performance for further decision making and performance optimization.
    3. Resolve conflicts and misunderstandings between office employees.
    4. Request Secretary for schedules and plans for various events, such as meetings, phone calls, etc.
    5. Assist Office Manager in conducting meetings and conferences.
    6. Act as a deputy of Office Manager.
    7. Provide leadership and guidance to teams.
    8. Motivate personnel through implementing employee development and motivation programs.

4. Secretary.

    1. Keep and coordinate schedules and agendas of all general and board meetings.
    2. Maintain and coordinate schedules of other events.
    3. Supply all authorized meeting attendees with copies of schedules and agendas.
    4. Ensure that all necessary supplies are ready for every upcoming meeting.
    5. Create and regularly update an annual schedule of general meeting, board meetings, and events.
    6. Design and maintain an annual list of planned events.
    7. Update and share a membership roster.
    8. Maintain and update other membership information.
    9. Make records and notes during meetings and other events.
    10. Maintain a guest log at meetings and other events.

5. Receptionist.

    1. Always look all right and be dressed as required by the company's dress code.
    2. Greet visitors and answer their questions politely.
    3. Type and design documents and papers.
    4. Fax and email electronic documents and letters.
    5. Coordinate and distribute all incoming mail and email.
    6. Assist secretary in making records during meetings and conferences.

6. General Clerk.

    1. Operate photocopiers, fax machines, scanners and other office equipment.
    2. Use computers and various software solutions to create and print out documents.
    3. Assist secretary in managing files and papers.
    4. Be in charge of all administrative support work.
    5. Sort and order documents and records.
    6. File papers through separating and sorting them along with similar files.

7. Payroll Clerk (Bookkeeper/Accountant).

    1. Keep paychecks accurate and up-to-date.
    2. Ensure that employees are paid on time.
    3. Keep paychecks accurate and up-to-date.
    4. Provides payroll information by answering questions and requests.
    5. Resolves payroll discrepancies by collecting and analyzing information.

All the people who work for a company need a clear idea of their job and their responsibilities. Everyone needs to know what to do, whom he or she is working with and who is going to tell him or her what to do. In other words, every company needs a system of organization.

In every small company, the system will be formal. The office staff will be told to do the task by the manager, and a secretary will look after the office business. Everyone understands what he or she has to do and the organization is very clear. In larger companies it is more difficult to explain things to people. The organization system must be more formal.

Assignment

1. A group of 4 members should conduct an interview to any two different types of companies. Learn how the organization was organized and know the different positions, and functions of their administrative officers and staffs.
2. The interview should be recorded/video. Make a report and be ready to present it in class.

THINGS TO THINK

Case Study - Employee Relations

Maria has been a secretary in your office for eleven years. The office atmosphere in the office is relaxed, friendly, and staff relationships are like as one big family.

Almost a year, you already observed that Maria got a lot personal calls on the telephone and even on her cell phone. She also spend time chatting with clientele and staff on non-related work subjects. One of your supervisor and two fellow workers complained to you that they think they are already affected with Maria's working style.

You decided to give Maria only a passing rate in her overall performance which means that she was below what should be expected on her. You are not sure how she will react to your addressing the situation. As Maria's manager, how will you handle this situation?

1. Meet with the manager to get specifics on the effect of Maria's behavior.
2. Have a meeting with Maria and discuss her behavior:
3. Remind Maria that she is a valued member of the team;
4. Explain your observation and explain how her time was wasted on personal matters that interfere with her work;
5. Explain the performance expectations ratings given to her;
6. Let her know that you will trust her to use her judgment to correct the situation on her own at this point, and reiterate your confidence in her performance

Case Study - Understanding Work Ethic

Bertha is a receptionist for the front lobby. As receptionist, she is responsible for making copies for the people in her office. Her son, Bert, comes in and needs some copies for a school project. He brought his own paper and needs 300 copies for his class. If he doesn't bring the copies with him, he will fail the project. The company copier does not require a security key, nor do they keep track of copies made by departments.

Identify the problem or ethical issue:

Bertha is tempted to make copies for personal use at her workplace.

What are the facts?

Bertha is a company employee entrusted with the use of office equipment and supplies. The copier is for office use.

What are your solutions to the problem?

LEARNING ASSESSMENT

SCORE _____

NAME_____ YEAR/SECTION_____ DATE_____

I. Questions and Answer. The following questions require a brief but complete explanation.

1. ABC Company is a partnership in Motorcycle Trading business having 5 partners with equal sharing of capital. The partnership is putting up an organizational chart and they agreed that they assign the right positions for themselves. Help the 5 partners to design an organizational chart, giving the right position for each of them.

    a. Minerva Reyes – BS-Accounting, License accountant with 5-year experience in the Accounting Department;
    b. Jho Villa – BS-Office Admin graduate, 2- year experience as insurance counselor.
    c. Juan Reyes – an entrepreneur, managing his own motorcycle supplies. A graduate of BS-Nursing but not practicing his profession.
    d. Lito Avior – BS-Accounting. 10 years in teaching.
    e. Liza Uy – BS-Management. Housewife. Had a 2 years' experience as a staff.

2. Which part of the following tasks is not for the bookkeeper?

    a. Keep paychecks accurate and up-to-date.
    b. Use computers and various software solutions to create and print out documents.
    c. Keep paychecks accurate and up-to-date.

3. Which of the following tasks is for the office manager?

    a. Be in charge of all administrative support work.
    b. Coordinate and distribute all incoming mail and email.
    c. Report senior management on office performance and issues.

4. List down at least 5 tasks of an administrative secretary.

5. List down at least 5 tasks of finance manager.

MODULE 4

ADMINISTRATIVE OFFICE PROCEDURES

The business maxim is: "Get organized, or get ready for trouble."

One way to view an office system is to look at it as an interconnected network of resources. This includes the physical layout of the office, supplies and equipment as well as the relationships between people, technologies and other business resources. All of these must work together well to achieve a smooth operating environment and successful outcomes.

Even if an office is ideally designed, it cannot function to its potential if the people do not know the policies and procedures so well. Objectives provide overall direction for making decisions, and office policies and procedures serve as mechanisms for their accomplishment. Coordinated efforts produce an atmosphere in which the manager's concern for every customer can be expressed to its maximum.

Definite office policies and carefully planned procedures are the pre-requisites for running a smooth and efficient office. This is the reason why every organization has administrative procedures.

Administrative procedures are a set or system of rules that govern the procedures for managing an organization. These procedures are meant to establish efficiency, consistency, responsibility, and accountability. They help establish the legitimacy of management action by ensuring the application of management rules and decisions is done in an objective, fair, and consistent manner. They help ensure that managers are held accountable for decisions that deviate from the procedures. There are no differences between administrative procedures in public and in private. Administrative procedures are part of nearly every public and private organization.

Policies and procedures. They are designed to influence and determine all major decisions and actions, and all activities take place within the boundaries set by them. Procedures are the specific methods employed to express policies in action in day-to-day operations of the organization. Together, policies and procedures ensure that a point of view held by the governing body of an organization is translated into steps that result in an outcome compatible with that view.

Office policies vary widely depending on the size of the office, staff abilities, and the personal philosophy of the office involved. Management selects those policies and procedures that lend themselves best to the training, time, and work habits.

Below are some of the terminologies that are usually discussed in the administrative manual, however, every organization have different approaches in their implementation.

Employee Recruitment and Selection Policy

It describes the process for attracting and selecting external job candidates. A recruitment policy can serve as a rubric that recruiters and hiring managers can use to create an effective hiring process :

Step 1: Identify Vacancy and Evaluate Need
Step 2: Develop Position Description
Step 3: Develop Recruitment Plan
Step 4: Select Search Committee
Step 5: Post Position and Implement Recruitment Plan

Step 6: Review Applicants and Develop Short List
Step 7: Conduct Interviews
Step 8: Select Hire
Step 9: Finalize Recruitment

Orientation

Orientation is the process use for a newly hired employee in the organization. The Human Resources department is the one handling this event to give the needed information to the newly hired. The subjects commonly discuss are in the areas of: job description of the employee; the compensation and the benefits; the organizational chart; to whom he is to work with-like his immediate manager and supervisor; the work environment; the safety of the work; the rules and regulations; the company history and its culture; and other information that is important to the company and to the employee.

The orientation is also for the new employee to feel that he is very much welcomed as a member of the organization. This will make any employee feel comfortable with the working environment.

Human Resources

The human resources department spearhead the orientation for new employees; conduct training for development; arrange meetings, and other events for the management and staff; review employees working performance; advices and give counseling.

Safety

Executive management with the office management recommend safety precautions to be observed by the organization:

anti-harassment policy; sexual abuse; confidentiality of documents; theft; and other administrative procedures. This safety is discussed to the new and old employees regularly to serve as a reminder.

Assessment

It is important to be clear to the employees that their performance is subject for assessment at the end of the year so that negativity on the part of the staff will be avoided. Assessment is an effective tool for managing employees' performance not only for the company to reach its objectives but for the employees to grow professionally.

Training and development.

Tests are used to find out whether employees have mastered training materials. They can help identify employees who might benefit from either remedial or advanced training.

Control

Clear communication of what your role entails in the company should be clear to the employees. Discuss your position, the required chain of command, and your expectations on their job performance; and the rules to follow with the consequences if violated. Build your trust and confidences with your staff by showing you are doing your best to perform your duties and responsibilities. Learn to identify problem employees and the best way to handle them. Avoid excessive control, let them feel and see you count on their abilities and decisions. Encourage staff to ask questions and offer feedback.

Promotion

Organizations may use tests to identify employees who possess managerial potential or higher level capabilities, so that these employees can be promoted to assume greater duties and responsibilities.

Daily Routines

- Office Hours
- Opening Routines
- Midday Routines
- Closing Routines

Homework

1. Get a copy of an Administrative Office Procedure Manual in one of the companies near your place. Of course, you must know somebody from that office to give or lend it to you.
2. Report to the class what is in the manual.

THINGS TO THINK

Case Study

"Frightening Behavior"

A supervisor contacts the Human Resources Office because one of his employees is making the other employees in the office uncomfortable. He said the employee does not seem to have engaged in any actionable misconduct but, because of the employer's new workplace violence policy, and the workplace violence training he had just received, he thought he should at least mention what was going on. The employee was recently divorced and had been going through a difficult time for over two years and had made it clear that he was having financial problems which were causing him to be stressed out. He was irritable and aggressive in his speech much of the time. He would routinely talk about the number of guns he owned, not in the same sentence, but in the same general conversation in which he would mention that someone else was causing all of his problems.

Exercise 2: "Helping Mary" Mary is a coworker in your agency. She has been a valuable employee to your group and one of the most respected experts in her field. You notice lately, though, that she is more reserved and is absent quite a bit. You hear her quietly crying or having a fight with someone on the phone frequently. She is a bit jumpy while she is at work, always looking over her shoulder when she goes somewhere. You ask her to lunch one day and voice your concern. Mary says she is having some problems at Home but there is nothing to worry about; she can handle them herself. Several weeks later you notice that Mary's fear has escalated. She rarely leaves the building. When she must leave, she moves quickly, always covering her face. She works erratic hours. Her fear is really beginning to affect everyone at work. You are all concerned for her but don't know what is going on. You begin to wonder if there is a real danger, both to Mary and tcher.

Question

1. Do you believe this is a situation that requires further action on your part? Why or why not?
2. What are the appropriate interventions in this situation? Think about those things that you and the other coworkers can do, what Mary's supervisor can do, what security staff can do, and what any other agency staff can do.
3. Are there other protections that should be considered for Mary and her coworkers?

LEARNING ASSESSMENT   SCORE _____

NAME_____ YEAR/SECTION_____ DATE_____

I. True or False. If false write the correct answer.

_____ 1. Daily routines are activities or tasks done every day.

_____ 2. Tasks to be done must be plan early in the morning before you start your day.

_____ 3. Tests are used to find out whether employees have mastered training materials.

_____ 4. Arrive in the office at least 15 minutes early so you can fix yourself and your table is included in the daily routines.

_____ 5. Start your day planning for big tasks instead of an easy one.

_____ 6. Control is assessing what tasks has been done for a day or for a year.

_____ 7. Assessment is identifying the problems as quickly as possible so remedy/remedies may apply.

_____ 8. Orientation is regarded as social or personal relationships that will make one familiar with the people working inside the office.

_____ 9. Office policies and procedures provide overall direction for making decisions, and

_____ 10. Policy serves as mechanisms for their accomplishment.

II. Define the following. 3 Points each.

1. Administration.

2. Office Procedures.

3. Office System.

4. Orientation.

5. Promotion

6. Policy.

7. Control.

8. Assessment.

9. Recruitment & Selection

MODULE 5

OFFICE SPACE PLANNING & ERGONOMICS

Office Space Planning is the process of organizing certain office furniture and office functions to work effectively together while using space efficiently.

An office is defined as a work area for handling information or a production area with data processing equipment. Office planning could then be defined as determining the arrangement of all physical components into a coordinated unit that can most effectively handle the volume of work and the type of information necessary to carry out a mission.

The Importance of Office Layout

1. Maximizing the productivity. There should be a sufficient level of office furniture and accessories that employees can use to increase employees' productivity.
2. Making sure that employees are given a workspace that they can call their own. An office cubicle or an office desk and chair give a high level of importance and foster a sense of 'place' in the company.
3. Ensuring that equipment is ergonomic and sound. It plays a part in the productivity of the employees and also in the customers. A customer is much more likely to return to a place if the office furniture in the reception

is aesthetically pleasing as opposed to shabby looking furniture.

Consideration on Planning an Effective Space Layout

1. The profile of the company
2. The type of work conducted by each department in the company
3. The needs of clients that visit the office
4. The extent to which furniture can facilitate interaction and the exchange of information between managers, employees, and clients.

Work Place Planning

The types of office accommodation will have a great impact to the employees because of its functionality and of its aesthetics and other ergonomics features. A physical environment that is visually pleasing makes employees inspired to work. There are factors that shape the environment and determine people's satisfaction with their workspace.

Thermal Comfort.

Thermal comfort means that a person wearing a normal amount of clothing feels neither too cold nor too warm. Every individual have their temperature preferences especially when there is always traffic in the workplace so there is no one temperature that can satisfy everyone. Nevertheless maintaining constant thermal conditions in the office is important.

Air quality

Studies show that pollutant levels can sometimes be higher indoors than those measured outside. Inadequate maintenance of ventilation systems can have the most significant impact on the condition of the air inside the office. It can be a source of odors or pollutants. Contaminants in the air can come from many sources, both inside and outside, examples are: dust, pollen, fungi, etc. A properly operating ventilation system and related air quality tools can reduce air pollution in an office

Lighting

Research discovered that exposure to natural light in an office space impacts employees' quality of life, like improves sleep, reduces eye fatigue and headaches and has a positive impact on health and well-being. Since the office cannot avoid using artificial light, a strategic plan is required to make sure light from the window can move throughout the space inside the office.

Ease of Interaction

In planning for an office design and space, the office goal should be considered. If your company wants to have an energetic, collaborative and friendly environment, an open office will help you to achieve it. Open offices are believed to have a better communication and teamwork.

Workspace cleanliness

The workplace environment influences employees' productivity, performance and well-being. According to Kimberly-Clark, break rooms have been found to have approximately

20,951 germs per square inch. Parts of the break room that tend to be touched the most, such as doorknobs, microwave oven handles and sinks, can be ripe with germs. Employers may want to clean these places on a frequent basis, and daily during flu season.

An occupational hazard is commonly caused by neglect on the part of the employer or a lack of awareness by workers. When the office or worksite is not clean, it may increase the chance that a hazard will go unnoticed by a supervisor and staff members.

Amount of space

When designing an office space, it's important to consider how easily employees can communicate with one another and upper management. Still to consider is the needs for quiet areas, private meetings and for some employees who might not do well with constant interruptions. Some companies have multi-faceted like providing an area for nursing mothers and a multi-purpose room that can facilitate large meetings or a group yoga session.

Comfort of furnishings

Having a diverse set of office furniture items assist towards employee wellbeing. As many office workers would be aware, taking regular short breaks away from their desks is fundamental especially if they want to avoid the development of uncomfortable back pains and other injuries.

What is Ergonomics?

Ergonomics is a scientific study of human works, specifically office environment. Ergonomics aims to improve workspaces and environments to minimize risk of injury or harm.

Some workers are weak and cannot adapt to a job that exceeds their body's physical limitations. This result to the so called Work-related Musculoskeletal Disorders (WMSD) that result to injury to the said person and time loss for the company. According to research, worker's compensation claims for injuries that occur in the office environment come from three areas – computer work, materials handling (lifting and carrying) and general office work.

To achieve best practice <u>design</u>, Ergonomists is use by the company in the following:

1. Chair. A chair should have a supports to the spinal curves. The height of the chair is fine if the feet rest flat on the floor, thighs are parallel to the floor. The armrests adjusted so the arms gently rest on them with your shoulders relaxed
2. Keyboard. The mouse should be place within easy reach and near the keyboard. While typing or using your mouse, keep wrists straight, upper arms close to the body, and hands at or slightly below the level of the elbows. If possible it is good when both handls can alternately use to operate the mouse by moving the mouse to the other side of your keyboard.
3. Laptops. This can run the risk of developing <u>musculoskeletal disorders</u> because the screen is too low for the person using it and this causes the user to jut out his/her neck. This result to improper posture, strain neck and the pressure of the weight of your head on your neck can cause it to permanently form. This results in a forward neck <u>posture</u>, with a rounded, hunched back.
4. Sitting For Too Long

Human bodies are not made to sit for many hours this will result to some sort of physical consequences such as <u>lower lumbar back pain</u>. Getting up and moving about every half an hour is a good practice just to give the move of the body in a variety of ways.

There are five main principles of ergonomics: safety, comfort, ease of use, productivity and performance and aesthetics.

Read, Think and Learn

Craig Stewart, ASP and co-owner of Kare Products, is an ergonomic specialist with 20 years of experience. Here are four different cases that Stewart evaluated and redesigned:

The corporate headquarters of a large medical company requested an analysis for one of its call center divisions. Nicknamed, "the dungeon," workers complained of noise, lack of space, dust, mold, physical discomfort, injuries, and general dissatisfaction.

Without initial consideration for functional design, this phone center underwent numerous modifications over two years. Cramped workstations led to shoulder and neck injuries and the poor panel layout of the "open" office created challenges for janitorial and IT personnel.

On top of a 15 percent ergonomic injury rate, high dispersion of dust and mold had the group of 30 workers complaining of allergies and colds. Supervisors spent much of their days having to address the complaints, and employee absenteeism spiked.

New height-adjustable desks eliminated shoulder and low back complaints. Each requires only ten minutes to adjust, reducing facilities costs for set up and re-design time.

A redesigned floor plan utilizes panels and tall filing cabinets to create privacy and act as a sound barrier during phone calls. Workstations cost less and provide more storage. To address air quality and environmental concerns, we incorporated materials such as sustainable woods with no VOC out gassing and water based glues.

The result: a clean and functional environment for employees. Complaints dropped from over four per day to zero. The department is happier, more efficient, and more productive.

Case No. 1;

In a high-rise office building, a division of employees complained about lack of privacy and excessive noise that interfered with their ability to complete their work. An increase in lost workdays and a rise in Workers' Compensation cases concerned the HR department.

Kare Products identified the need for a single overall design to accommodate both group interactions as well as individual workstations.

A paneling system allows easy interface with co-workers for group projects in an isolated space, reducing noise. Sit stand desk configurations with dual height adjustable monitor arms address ergonomic injuries. Modular design allows the company to reconfigure, expand, or move easily.

Green furniture with water based glues, recycled laminates and non-toxic paints create a healthier workplace. When asked, employees appreciated how uniquely each workstation fit their needs, as well as the aesthetic appeal.

Case No. 3 Medical Call Center (Office)

One medical company needed ergonomics so much that its employees had begun to refer to its offices as "the dungeon." Reports from the site demonstrate how conditions had become almost unworkable: loud noise, cramped workspaces, dust, mold, and repetitive work tasks led to extreme discomfort among employees, who suffered a staggering 15 percent ergonomic injury rate. The worst of the conditions appeared in the company's call center, where irregular updates and renovations made without a long-term employee wellness strategy, created major problems for workers. An open office layout led to extremely tight workstations, which contributed to neck and shoulder injuries while preventing janitorial and IT staff from doing their jobs effectively. Worse still, the call center employees suffered allergies and other illnesses, leading to a major uptick in absenteeism.

After an ergonomic assessment, the company instituted several changes to improve the ergonomic quality of the work environment. Shoulder and neck injuries vanished after height-adjustable desks were installed, and a new floor plan created greater privacy and added much-needed storage space for the workers, improving morale and productivity. Finally, the company introduced sustainable woods to eliminate volatile organic compounds (VOCs) in the air, which helped to address the high rate of employee illness.

The end result was a reduction in complaints from four per day to zero.

Case No. 4 Die Cast Plant (Manufacturing)

Another company saw its productivity double after ergonomic improvements were implemented. A die cast manufacturing plant in central Ohio enjoyed major financial rewards after investing in ergonomic solutions, with a one-time cost of $495,500 that spurred annual benefits of $1,910,000 over a span of ten years.

The factory had already implemented some ergonomic solutions for its workers, but further analysis led to even greater improvements. In fact, objective analysis is the cornerstone of any ergonomics program. Once you have collected both subjective and objective data, it's time to take a step back and assess what you've learned so far. Is there injury risk at this job?

What is the level of risk? How can the risk be reduced?

Improvements at this factory included pallet lifts to reduce the time employees spent bent over carrying weights, which dramatically reduced back and shoulder conditions among workers. With a full ergonomics program, the plant reported major improvements in virtually all financial categories, with workers' compensation costs dropping by 93 percent, absenteeism falling by 67 percent, and productivity rising by 54 percent. It's a perfect example of how minor changes, including healthy workstation design and a careful understanding of the physical tasks that lead to injuries, can dramatically change the human and financial outlook of an organization.

Case Study #3: Deere and Company (Manufacturing)

A final example of how ergonomics can reshape a workplace occurred at Deere and Company, the well-known farm equipment manufacturer. This case study illustrates the necessity of including your workers in the early stages of an ergonomics program. The workplace athletes performing the job each and every day are uniquely qualified to help you assess the job. They are the experts at their job. Involving them in the assessment process can generate helpful improvement ideas and gets the workplace athlete's buy-in early on. They are much more likely to adopt changes to their work environment down the road if you involve them early and often.

At Deere and Company, assessors recommended changes in the construction department that would limit the physical toll taken on workers performing their routine tasks. Analysis and feedback from workers showed that lifting heavy objects was common, while poorly designed tools contributed to repetitive motion injuries. Further, observation revealed that Deere and Company was losing money on reduced productivity due to the work environment. Workers' compensation costs increased by 15 percent each year, and high numbers of first-aid cases led to staggering health care costs and huge losses in productivity due to absenteeism.

However, a new ergonomics training program helped Deere and Company to reduce their injury rates and provide a healthier work environment for its employees. The course covered common issues, many of which appear at companies across industries. Are there any heavy or strenuous lifting/lowering tasks in the job? Do the hand tools they use have an awkward grip? Is the height of the work comfortable for them? Do they experience fatigue and discomfort doing the job? These questions were addressed and the root problems corrected with redesigned workspaces and new hand tools to help workers avoid strains and stress injuries.

After implementation, Deere and Company reported an 83 percent reduction in back injuries, along with a 32 percent drop in health care compensation over the last ten years. By involving workers early in the process, the company came to understand the issues on its job floor and learned to address them in detail.

Conclusion

These case studies demonstrate not only the power of an ergonomic plan—they also illustrate how engaging directly with employees and understanding the challenges they face can inform a successful ergonomics program. Working with employees for their own health empowers them to take charge of their wellness, leading to a supportive workplace culture and a workforce that stays on the job without interruption and monetary loss.

Class Activity

Divide the students into four groups: assign each group to a room where one group can be allowed to decorate walls without arranging the furniture. The other one can decorate walls and allow to arrange the furniture but they have to conform to rules that the teacher will give. The third group is allow to decorate walls, arrange the furniture without any rules to conform with, The last group is not allow to do any decoration and rearranging of furniture, but only to clean the room.

Report the outcome of the activity according to the ambiance, organization and productivity of the group.

LEARNING ASSESSMENT   SCORE _____

NAME_____YEAR/SECTION_____DATE_____

I. Identification.

1. _____ is a physical factor within the environment that harms the musculoskeletal system.
2. _____ is the process of designing or arranging workplaces, products and systems so that they fit the people who use them.
3. _____ are becoming more than just places where employees can eat their lunch – they facilitate interaction, aid creativity, and encourage spontaneity.
4. _____ is the process of organizing certain office furniture and office functions to work effectively together while using space efficiently.
5. An _____ is defined as a work area for handling information.

II. List down what is being ask on the following questions. Provide good reasons in doing so. Use the space provided. 5 points for each question.

   A. What are the considerations that an administrative officer would think of when planning an space layout?
   B. If the administrative officer would consider to have an ergonomics workplace what are the benefits that everybody will gain.

MODULE 6

DEALING WITH VISITORS

Members of your organization or the public may visit your office to get information or assistance from you. It is important to receive them properly. Greet and find out how you can help or assist them. Visitors should feel they are welcome and treated with respect.

Personal Contact

Here are some simple things to do to make a favorable and professional impression with office guests.

1. Have a space where visitors can wait - a small room or just seats in the front office.
2. Make sure the reception area is always clean and tidy.
3. Put reading material on current affairs and brochures in the reception area.
4. Provide water and cups for visitors.
5. If it will take a long time before someone can be attended to, tell them how long they will have to wait.
6. If they cannot wait, take a message for the person they wanted to see.

When visitors visit a business environment, their first point of contact will be the person at reception, or at least the person who meets and greets. The first impression always makes a difference and presenting a positive image of you and the organization is very important. Dress and present yourself neatly. Stick to the dress code of the organization. Smile, maintain eye contact, listen, be positive and do your best to help them with their queries.

The importance of practicing professionalism in dealing with office visitors aim to:

    a. It creates a feeling of confidence in the visitor.
    b. The visitors get a positive impression about the organization.
    c. It helps build trust between the organization and its customers and employees.
    d. It attracts quality clients which will improve the business for the organization thereby increasing profit of the organization.

Telephoning

It is a must that everyone in the office exhibits a professional image, both in person and on the telephone. Give priority to incoming calls rather than the extension users. If the extension is engaged, give the caller the choice whether to hold or call back later. Keep the caller (who are holding and waiting for your next respond) informed as to what is happening by regularly going back to him.

The following phone tips should always be followed.

1. Answer the phone at once. Always identify the company and yourself properly. The standard greeting is - "San Juan Legal Office, Good morning. This is Riza speaking. How can I help you?"
2. If the caller is asking for something that you need time to reach for it, your respond is "Just a moment" and place the caller on hold.
3. Always make sure that there is a pen and a paper to write on in getting the message. Include the caller's name, time

and date, reason for the call, and call-back number. Some offices use a Message slip in getting in-coming calls.

Message Slip

Call Time _____ Date _____
To _____

While you were out

Name of Caller_____
Company of _____
Phone No. _____
Reason for Calling:_____

Messge _____

Action Taken_____

Taken by:_____

---

4. Speak clearly. Avoid using slang word and this includes "ok". Say figures in pairs – they are easier to understand. Say "29 - 76 - 84." Never answer the telephone while eating or drinking. The person on the other line cannot see the caller but hear. It will be best to take time to speak clearly, slowly with a cheerful tone of voice. Professionalism in answering the phone is very important. Use normal tone of voice when answering a call.
5. Address the caller properly by his or her title unless the caller is very familiar to you and had asked you to call him his first name. Still, it is proper to be polite.

ADMINISTRATIVE PROCEDURES AND MANAGEMENT

6. Listen carefully to the Caller. Repeat the information back to the caller when taking a very important message. Ask the caller to spell out difficult names.
7. Always be patient and helpful. Refer the caller to the right person if the call is not intended for you. There are three options for you.

   a. Explain that you will transfer his call.
      "Hold the line for a moment, I will transfer you to customer relations department."
   b. See if someone else can help.
   c. Ask the caller to ring back later

8. Always focus on the call. If someone in the office tries to interrupt you while you are on a call, politely remind them that you will attend to them as soon as you are finished.
9. Never leave the person on hold for more than a few seconds or they may become upset and hang up.
10. End the call by saying "Thank you for calling."
11. If you are the caller, let the other person hang up first.

7. **Different Types of Calls**

   1. *Routine Calls*

   Consider every call special. There is no routine calls. Always answer the call politely and with eagerness to help.

   2. *Calls that can resolve by the secretary/staff.*

   The secretary actually is the frontline person to accept all calls intended in their unit or office. Scrutinize calls that are not familiar before giving it to the executive.

The following are some examples of typical questions that can be resolved by an alert staff:

Staff: How can I help you?
Caller: I would like to speak with Atty. Castro
Staff: If you wish to make an appointment or reserve time for a consultation, I can help you. I have Atty. Castro's appointment book here at my desk.
Caller: Is Atty. Castro a practicing lawyer?
Staff: Yes, he is handling criminal cases.
Staff: Atty. Castro will be happy to discuss fees with you. If you wish to arrange a special consultation prior to your appointment, he can see you either next Monday at 10 o'clock in the morning or Wednesday at 3 o'clock in the afternoon. Which do you prefer?

3. **When the manager is not in the office**

It will be wise if the asst. administrator will always ask the manager of his whereabouts when leaving the office so that if one of the caller is an executive of the company you can tell exactly where the manager is. However, not all callers need to know the exact location of the manager. You can simply state, "Dr. Cruz is out of the office and is scheduled to be back by 2 o'clock this afternoon."

4. **Problem Calls**

   4.1 The Mystery Caller

A caller who refuses to provide adequate identification is called mystery caller because a legitimate person will identify themselves. If a mystery caller demands to speak directly with the executive, the secretary should politely remind the caller of the procedures to be observed before giving the call to the executive, and that his identity should be revealed.

4.2 The Indistinct Caller

If the caller cannot be heard clearly, use extra tact and courtesy by telling to give his number so you can call him back.

4.3 The Inquisitive Caller

Sometimes a caller may seek information, unless the staff is absolutely positive about the caller's identity, she can definitely provide information that is not confidential.

4.4 The "Nuisance" Caller.

Callers who call back again and again just to ask for an information that is confidential. Or a caller who ask for the executive to sell his product is nuisance caller. A skilled asst. administrator or secretary should deal with these callers in a professional manner.

5. **Follow-up Calls.**

A follow up calls should not be overlooked. One important function of a secretary is the follow up of an appointment made by callers or to follow up the calls of your executive. A note of the calls for follow up should always be check until it has been done.

6. **Personal Calls.**

Office staff should be trained to keep personal calls brief during office hours if it cannot be avoided. Personal calls of staff should be limited to emergencies and made as brief as possible.

Classroom Activity

You have learned the different types of calls. The class can have a short presentation on how the different calls can be handled by a professional administrative staff.

LEARNING ASSESSMENT

SCORE _____

NAME_____ YEAR/SECTION_____ DATE_____

Listing down what is ask of you and give a short note on it.

A. Why is it a must for any administrative staff to practice professionalism in dealing with people visiting or transacting business in the workplace? 5 points

B. Give pointers in the proper handling of calls. 10 points

C. Look at this message and then answer the questions.

Message for   Date: *July 20, 2019* Time: *10:00 am*
To: *Mr. Roger Reyes*
From: *Lita Cruz*   Tel. no. *501-304-222*
Message:
    Want you to call back in the afternoon of 4:00 pm

Signed: *AnnaMarie*

Question

1. Who call to talk to Mr. Roger Reyes on July 20, 1019?
2. Who wrote the message for Mr. Reyes?
3. Whose telephone number is 501-304-222
4. When Mr. Roger gets the message, what must he do?

MODULE 7

CORRESPONDENCE

Letters sent or received in the office is called correspondence or is refer to "Mail". Those letters, parcels, telegrams, internal memos, fax, e-mail, text messages or SMS (Short Message Service) and other documents are mail or correspondence.

The secretary or the assistant administrator in a small office is usually responsible in collecting and sorting mail or correspondence. In a big company, the receptionist takes this kind of responsibility where she stamped with date and time it was received and then put in mail boxes of different department for distribution The one in-charged for getting mail see to it that mails are collected in the morning and in the afternoon. If mail is "urgent" in nature the receptionist will call the office to get it at once.

Incoming Mail

The secretary need to organize all mails according to importance. The newspapers is place on top of the table, and mails arranged according to importance are place in the "in coming mail" basket. "Out going" mail is for all mails that are already seen and read by the manager. However, incoming mail marked "personal" or "confidential" should be put on the table on top of the newspaper.

Sorting and Processing

Normally, the secretary opened all mails but not those with marked "personal" and "confidential'. It is the responsibility of a secretary to sort the mail, slit the envelopes, remove and open the contents flat, attach the contents with a paperclip, stamp letters with a dater, and stack the mail in an orderly fashion. There is usually no reason to retain the envelope unless the letter does not contain a return address or if the addresses do not match. If it is absent or does not match, the envelope's corner imprint can be cut from the envelope and taped to the letter.

Mail Sorting. Most managers do not like their mail screened, but they do like it sorted. Following is a common **priority order for mail sorting:**

1. Registered letters
2. Special delivery letters
3. Express mailings
4. First-class professional mail
5. First-class business mail
6. Newsletters
7. Third-class circulars
8. Newspapers
9. Journals
10. Magazines
11. Catalogs

The incoming first-class mail is subdivided into three piles:

1. those letters that require the attention of someone outside the office staff;
2. those that require the manager's personal attention; and
3. those that require an staff/secretary's attention.

Enclosures.

When the mail is opened, and notice that a letter refers to an enclosure that is not enclosed, notify the manager or if the sender is known, immediately call their office that the supposed enclosure is not included in the letter.

The Holding File.

There are correspondence requesting reports, insurance statements, and others, that cannot be replied to immediately. These are place in a folder with a caption "holding files" until the request can be fulfilled. A holding file is also a constant reminder of the status of its contents.

Mechanics and Style

The letter to be sent is usually judge by its appearance and the quality of paper used. The acceptable style of letter should be thought accordingly and appropriate to the receiver. A letter's content, tone, and grammar will often determine a favorable or unfavorable response.

A standard business letter format most widely used for business letters are the following

1. *Full Block Style*. The text of the entire letter is justified left. The text is single spaced, except for double spaces between paragraphs. Margins 1.25 inch or pick your choice in the page layout of your computer as the default setting for most word-processing programs.
2. *Block Style*. The text of the entire letter is justified except for the date, inside address, complementary closing, name and signature. The text is single spaced, except for double spaces between paragraphs.

3. **Modified Block.** It resembles the block style, only the first line of each paragraph is indented five space from the left.

Punctuation Style

Two forms of punctuation may be used in the opening and closing lines of business letter: open and mixed (standard) punctuations. Of the two, the most commonly used is the mixed form.

1. **Open Format.** There is no punctuation after the salutation and no punctuation after the complementary closing. The full block and the block style are appropriate to use with open punctuation format.
2. **Mixed (Standard) Format.** The salutation is followed by a colon and the complementary closing is followed by a comma. In a letter that is strictly social or personal, the salutation is comma not a colon. Mixed punctuation is used in any letter styles.

Common Components and Formats

Heading. The heading contains the writer's address and the date of the letter.

Inside address. The inside address shows the name and address of the recipient of the letter. Always include title names (such as Dr.) if you know them.

Salutation. The salutation (or greeting) in a business letter is always formal. It often begins with "Dear {Person's name}." Once again, be sure to include the person's title if you know it (such as Ms., Mrs., Mr., or Dr). The salutation always ends with a colon.

Subject or reference line. A subject line is not really necessary. You may want to use one, however, so that the reader immediately knows what your letter is about. There are three common methods to distinguish the subject line from the body of the letter:

> Use "Subject:" or "Re:"
> Type the subject in bold letters
> Type the subject in capital letters

Body of the letter. The body is the meat of your letter, single space and left justify each paragraph. Be sure to leave a blank line between each paragraph. Be sure to also skip a line between the salutation and the body, as well as the body and the close.

Complimentary close. The complimentary close is a short and polite remark that ends your letter. The close begins at the same justification as your date and one line after the last body paragraph. Capitalize the first word of your closing (Very truly yours,) and leave four lines for a signature between the close and the sender's name. A comma should follow the closing.

Signature line. Skip at least four lines after the close for your signature, and then type out the name to be signed. This often includes a middle initial, although it is not required. The signature should be in blue or black ink.

Enclosures. If you have any enclosed documents, such as a resume, you can indicate this by typing "Enclosures" one line below the listing. You also may include the name of each document.

Enclosures should be clipped to a letter requiring signature unless they are quite bulky.

The Quality of Effective Letter

1. Clearness. Clear writing means that your reader will understand readily. Avoid all ambiguity, vagueness and possible doubts. Only one idea should be presented. Write simply and directly.

2. Conciseness. It is presenting the idea in a short possible words without sacrificing the completeness of meaning.
3. Correctness. The letter should be correct in physical make-up, free from all errors in punctuation and capitalization, in word usage, in grammar, and paragraph structure.
4. Concreteness. Use specific and concrete words that create a picture in your reader's mind. Avoid abstract and general terms.
5. Cheerfulness. The letter should suggest friendliness, confidence, helpfulness and optimism. It is polite and courteous. It says nothing that can offend the reader. The spirit is spontaneous.
6. Courtesy. Is a mental attitude, a point of view that implies respect, consideration, and helpfulness. Expression like 'thank you' and 'please' are always appreciated when they are used sincerely not mechanically.
7. Consideration. This is emphasizing the attitude of the Writer. 'You' attitude means writing from the point of view of the reader rather than from the writer's point of view.
8. Character. If the writer would like to infuse his letter with his personality, choose words carefully and arrange them in original phrases.

LEARNING ASSESSMENT   SCORE _____

NAME_____YEAR/SECTION_____DATE_____

I. True or False. Write true if the statement is correct, if false write the correct answer opposite the word false.

_____ 1. The quick and convenient way to relay daily business message is through business letter.

_____ 2. 'junk' mail is the mail the executive want to see first.

_____ 3. Incoming mail marked "personal" or "confidential" should not be opened by a third party.

_____ 4. The text is type double spaced, and provide double spaces between paragraphs.

_____ 5. Registered mail is regarded as priority mail.

_____ 6. 'Courtesy' shows that the writer is writing from the point of view of the reader and not from the writer's point of view.

_____ 7. Open punctuation is no punctuation after the salutation and a comma after the complementary closing.

_____ 8. In a modified block letter style, all lines are placed at the extreme left of the letter.

_____ 9. A "holding files" serve as a reminder of the request that are still pending.

_____ 10. The salutation that is followed by a colon and the complementary closing followed by a comma is using the standard punctuation style.

II. Listing down

A. List down the 7 common parts of body of a letter. Explain each part.

B. List down the 8 qualities of an effective letter

C. List the 8 mails received in the office and sort according to its importance.

MODULE 8
RECORDS MANAGEMENT SYSTEM

Records Management ensures that all types of files – including both physical and electronic – are kept safe and preserved and easily accessible when needed. However, those non-essential records are discarded in a timely manner according to established guidelines. Records provide evidence of the business activities and function.

Records management is the supervision and administration of digital or paper records. The record officer who created, received, maintained, used and disposed records are part of his records management duty.

Many of the files are currently created by electronics, but offices have to deal with paper files, too. It is important that the record officer should always analyze and screen material immediately upon receipt.

Paper records may be stored in boxes or on vertical filing cabinet, at a storage facility like vault for very important records or documents. Digital records may be stored on storage media in-house or in the cloud.

Records can be in paper, digital or other formats. Some examples include: emails, reports, databases, minutes of meetings, letters, photographs, stocks certificate, financial statements, legal documents: affidavit, real estate taxes, maps and other important papers of the company.

Importance of Records Management

Business records are kept so that they may be found and used when needed. It is expected that the one handling the records of the company can locate the files immediately, know the filing equipment and supplies, how to charge out, transfer and dispose of materials. Business records are the life-blood of the organization so that careful handling of those records are very important.

1. Efficiency of working since accessibility of documents is easy when needed.
2. Records provide evidence of the business activities and functions, and accountability.
3. Saves time because documents are retrieve easily.
4. Reduce space since you discard files that is non-essential to the business anymore.

It is vital that every business develops and maintains a record-keeping policy because the manner, in which records are filed, organized and retrieved impacts profitability, customer service and legal compliance.

Types of filing System

There are two general filing systems popular in the offices: alphabetical indexing and numerical indexing. Of the two, alphabetical indexing is the most popular in small and medium-size practices.

1. Alphabetical Indexing
Most offices file strictly alphabetically by individual last name or subject of the topic to be filed. In large volume practices where several individuals may have the same name, customers' records are filed by case number and the individual's number

is cross-indexed to an alphabetical list that incorporates the customer's address. It is not unusual in large practices to have several individuals with the name Mary E. Garcia or Juan Jose. Regardless of the system used, guides should be used to divide the drawers into appropriate sections, and folders or pockets should be used to hold all records of the customer or topic.

2. Numerical Indexing

Numerical indexing is sometimes used in large practices conducted by several doctors/managers/supervisors and assistants. In a numerical indexing system, identifying numbers are used on the file folders that are arranged numerically. The advantages of this system are those of fast and more accurate refilling, the opportunity for indefinite expansion, and confidentiality.

After each individual name is assigned a case number, said folder is labeled by the number and this is followed by the three-unit alphabetical system (eg, 1476 - Juan, Jose L). A small cross-index card must also be prepared that contains the same information in reverse (eg, Juan, Jose L - 1476). This card is filed alphabetically in a separate file, and the case records are filed by number in the master file. Numerical indexing also requires a log book that lists each number assigned so that the same number will not be assigned to different clients/patients. The extra steps involved in this system offer few advantages over the simpler alphabetical system. It is more appropriate for businesses that have thousands of active accounts.

Filing Rules for Proper Alphabetizing

Rule 1: Name of individuals are transposed when filed as follows:
last name first name or initial then middle name or initial.

As written it is filed By Unit, before filing alphabetically. For example:

John W. Cruz   Betty S. Perez   Tomas R. Maximo

Sergio O. Lopez

Unit 1	Unit 2	Unit 3	Unit 4
Cruz	John	W.	
Lopez	Sergio	O.	
Maximo	Tomas	R.	
Perez	Betty	S.	

Rule 2: Surnames which include prefixes such as D', Da, De, Del, De la, Della, Den, Des, Di, Du, El, Fitz, L', La, Las, Le, Les, Lo, Los, M', Mac, Mc, O', Saint, St., Ste., Te, Ten, Ter, Van, Van der, Von, etc. are filed as one word in alphabetical order. For example:

D' Genoa de Silva   Peter Mac Gregor   Saint Thomas De Leon

Ma.Cecilia Trinidad

Unit 1	Unit 2	Unit 3
De Leon	Saint Tomas	
De Silva	D'Genoa	
Mac Gregor	Peter	
Trinidad	Ma. Cecilia	

Rule 3: When it is impossible to distinguish the first or last name, or if confusion lies in the arrangement of a name, it is filed as it is written with the last name as the first filing unit while creating a cross-reference from the first name. For example: Pas Boss Solidarity, Cheng Kai Sek Hospital, Pektak Cho League.

Unit 1	Unit 2	Unit 3	Unit 4
Cheng Kai Sek	Hospital		
Pas Boss	Solidarity		
Petak Cho	League		

Rule 4: Hyphenated and compound last names are treated as one unit. Ignore the hyphen and file the two words as one unit. Example: Dianne Roger-Bach, Mark St. Paul, Louie Villa-De Vega

Unit 1	Unit 2	Unit 3	
Roger-Bach	Dianne		
St. Paul	Mark		
Villa-De Vega	Louie		

Rule 5: A. Titles which are intrinsic part of the name are considered as the first unit. For example: Sister Theresa, Father Burgo, Prince Charles

Unit 1	Unit 2	Unit 3	
Father Burgo			
Prince Charles			
Sister Theresa			

B. When title of a person is added to a full name, it should be considered as the last unit. For example: Father Terry Shields. Colonel George Sabas, Mayor James Paras,

Unit 1	Unit 2	Unit 3	
Paras	James	Mayor	
Sabas	George	Colonel	
Shields	Terry	Father	

C: Other titles and appendages such as Sr., Jr., II, Mrs., Ph. D., are also considered as the last name. Example: James A. Baker, II, John A. Baker III, Mark G. Spilmon, Jr., Michael E. Chan, Ph. D.

Unit 1	Unit 2	Unit 3	Unit 4
Baker	James	A.	II
Baker	John	A.	III
Chan	Michael	E.	Ph.D
Spilmon	Mark	G.	Jr.

D: Firm names beginning with a title should be indexed and filed as written. For example: Dr. Pepper Bottling Co.; Doctor Pepper Bottling Company, McDonnald Refreshing Juice

Unit 1	Unit 2	Unit 3	Unit 4
McDonnald	Refreshing	Juice	
Doctor	Pepper	Bottling	Company
Dr. Pepper	Bottling	Co.	

Rule 6: All Abbreviations in names should be alphabetized as though they were spelled out. For Example: St. Charles Review Ctr. ; Acme Mfg. Co.; Ft. Bonifacio

Unit 1	Unit 2	Unit 3	Unit 4
Acme	Manufacturing	Company	
Fort	Bonifacio		
Saint	Charles	Review	Center

Rule 7: A business name is filed as written unless it is the name of an individual, in that case it should be transposed. Example: Cecilia Lopez Store, Ace Hardware, Ben B. Soto Film.

Unit 1	Unit 2	Unit 3	Unit 4
Ace	Hardware		
Lopez	Cecilia	Store	
Soto	Ben	B.	Film

The exception to this rule is when a firm named for an individual is so well know that to transpose it would cause confusion. In that case it is filed as written. For example: Marshall Field & Co., Smith Bell & Company, Henry Ford Memorial

Unit 1	Unit 2	Unit 3
Henry	Ford	Memorial
Marshall	Field &	Company
Smith	Bell &	Company

Rule 8: When a business name is made up of two or more surnames, it is filed as written - with each name considered as a separate unit. For example: Perez Perez Law Office; Sam and Samson Bakery;

Unit 1	Unit 2	Unit 3	Unit 4
Perez	Perez	Law	Office
Sam and	Samson	Bakery	

Rule 9: Hyphenated Words and Names. A hyphenated name is filed as one unit. Example: Use-N-Save Company; Top-Choice Meats Company;

Unit 1	Unit 2	Unit 3	Unit 4
Top-Choice	Meats	Company	
Use-N-Save	Company		

Rule 10: When letters are used together to form a name, each letter is considered as a separate unit. As Written As Filed By Unit 1 2 3 4. Example: AA Driving School, ABC Engineering, WGN Company,

Unit 1	Unit 2	Unit 3	Unit 4
A	A	Driving	School
A	B	C	Engineering
W	G	N	Company

Rule 11.

   A. The 's when used to designate a possessive is disregarded since it denotes possession, but does not alter the name. As Written As Filed By Unit: Teal's Garden Store
   B. The apostrophe designating the possessive following a plural is disregarded. The "s" is part of the word and is considered. As Written As Filed By Unit. What's New Online Whats New Online
   C. The 's when used to designate a possessive is disregarded since it denotes, Men's Club

   Unit 1

Teal	Garden	Store
Whats	New	Online
Mens	Clug	

Rule 12: In general articles, conjunctions, and prepositions are not considered when filing.

   A. An article that begins a name is disregarded, Example: The Last Stop Motel; A Nice Place.

B. Disregard conjunctions, articles and prepositions that are part of the name. Example: Stop & Go Groceries; Top of the World Bar.
C. Prepositions that begin a name are considered as part of the name. By Womens Designs On the Pier.

Last	Stop	Motel (The)	
Nice	Place	Motel (A)	
Stop (&)	Go	Groceries	
Top (of the)	World	Bar	
By	Womens	Designes	
On (the)	Pier	Lighthouse	

Rule 13: Consideration of numeric names.

A. Numeric names are always filed as though spelled out.
B. Numbers of more than two digits are given their proper numeric value. Example: 900 Club, 10th Floor Lounge, 5000 Cornell Apts.

Nine	Hundred	Club	
Tenth	Floor	Lounge	
Five	Thousand	Cornel	Apartments

Rule 14: In geographic names where there is more than one word, each word is to be considered as a separate unit. Names with a prefix are considered as one unit. Example: North East Bank, North West Publishers, Northeast Transit Co.

Cross reference can be used for clarification.

North	East	Bank	
North	West	Publishers	
Northeast	Transit	Company	

Rule 15: Company names where part of the names is abbreviated, spell it in full. Example: Pan Pacific Ltd. Del Norte Safe Co., Mississippi Corp. Camp Club, LLC.

Unit 1	2	3
Pan	Pacific	Limited
Del Norte	Safe	Company
Mississippi	Corporation	
Camp	Club	Limited Liability Company

Rule 16: Institutions and organizations are filed under the significant word or location. Example: Hotel Palawan, Hotel Palawan Restaurant, First Savings Bank of Manila, University of Rizal.

Unit 1	2	3	4
Palawan	Hotel		
Palawan	Hotel	Restaurant	
Manila	First	Savings	Bank (of)
Rizal	University (of)		

Rule 17: Names of governmental units are filed under the name of the location or political division by the significant word or title. Example: Malabon City Collector, Makati Dept. of Welfare, Philippines Dept. of Defense.

Unit 1	2	3
Malabon	City	Collector
Makati	Department (of)	Welfare
Philippines	Department (of)	Defense

Rule 18: When filing bank names, first file under the city and their location and then use the name of the bank as written. Example: Second National Bank of Makati, Sampaloc Rural Bank in Manila, Hongkong Shanghai Bank

Unit 1	2	3	4
Makati	Second	National	Bank (of)
Manila (in)	Sampaloc	Rural	Bank
Hongkong	Shanghai	Bank	

Note: From rule 1 to rule 18, consider to arrange the names alphabetically after arranging them by units.

Alphabetic filing system is the basic filing systems.

Numeric Filing System

A numeric filing system classify materials using numbers as headings. This system is used for purchase orders, checks, and other records that have a unique number assigned to each document. Numeric filing system also uses the alphabetic filing systems. Example Rodriguez is the first customer in the company where the number 001 is allotted to Rodriguez, all the papers relating to him is placed in file No: 001. Likewise, in looking for Rodriguez folder, one will first refer in the alphabetic file records where specific numbers are filed according to the individual names Usually the individual names are recorded in the index files or record book arranged alphabetically.

The Subject File

If the subject is important, the information is better filed by subject in an alphabetically indexed file. For example 'Employee' Complaints is the subject, individual folders with employee's name may follow after the subject title A brief sampling of subject file titles is:

    Employees' Complaint   (subject/title)
        Ferrer, Ruben
        Perez, Liza
        (other individual folders)
    Insurance   (subject/title)
        Malayan Insurance Company
        Grepalife Insurance Company
        (other companys' folders)

Index Cards.

Index card is use to cross-reference files that are in the vertical files or somewhere, that access to it will takes time to retrieve. It comes in different sizes, and are kept in a box that is larger than the index card. An index card is usually preferred in extensive filing systems as it is more readily kept up to date. It is also use in writing short notes and getting messages over the phone

Color Coding

Color coding is for different categories of customers. The use of color coding depends on the choice of the office. Plain manila folders with a colored stickers or labeling the folder tab placed at the edge of the folder to subdivide files from different categories. The use of bold colors for every division will stand out in the filing cabinet for easier access for files. Below are the examples.

    Folders from ABCD is colored Red
    Folders from EFGH is colored Green
    Folders from IJKL is colored Blue
    Folders from MNOP is colored Orange

Or color coding by subjects:

Office Correspondence - Green (followed by individual files)

Financial Records - Red (followed by individual files)

Stock Certificates - Blue (followed by individual or companys' folder)

The use of color coding also speeds retrieval and reduces misfiling.

Cross-Reference Sheets

A cross-reference is the recommended when the documents contain two or more names or subject titles that are closely related or is connected to two or more departments. The original document should be reproduce. For example in a subject file under "Cases of Employees Absences." This could be filed under the subject file of "Employees" and cross-referenced under "Absences", or "Cases".

A cross-reference filing system is necessary for a numerical indexing system and a subject file. Each can contribute to an efficient filing system.

Pulled Files

When the secretary pulls records in the filing cabinet and gave it to the manager, she should mark or note it in the cross-reference of that file.

Tickler Files

A well-organized tickler file is helpful in keeping special notations and memoranda in order. The file is usually a small container holding a card or index card. The cards are separated by tab dividers for each month and subdivided for each day of the current month.

The tickler files is use for notations of information such as appointment reminders, approaching due dates for birthdays, seminars or other events, insurance premiums or taxes, subscription expirations, and other reminders of what should be done for a day. The tickler files should be reviewed daily in order not to miss any of the reminders that are noted on the said file.

Filing Equipment

Different Filing equipment comes in a large variety of styles and sizes:

1. Vertical drawer cabinets –

The vertical drawer is the most popular and commonly used by most of the offices, but it consumer more floor spaces, more time to access the files, and more expensive. It stored about 100 inches of files. The vertical files is beneficial to store confidential files since it can be locked.

2. Open Shelving

Company with a centralized system of filing used this open shelves filing system. It saves on floor space and money. The design of the open shelves depends, either stationary or mobile (a rollers are attached to the bottom). This is a common use in library since it is similar to a bookcase. Open shelving saves on space and has 80 percent more capacity. For mobile shelving it can be placed in higher density and offers 405 percent more capacity than cabinets.

3. Lateral cabinets –

Used in some offices as an alternative to vertical drawer cabinets. They have essentially the same limitations as vertical cabinets, although they can provide some space savings as well as retrieval efficiency. A 5 drawer lateral cabinet occupies approximately 6.8 square feet of floor space and holds almost 2.5 times more than a vertical drawer cabinet. The lateral cabinet can be seen most in medical offices and dental clinics.

The Active/Inactive Files

There are two categories of records, the active files and the inactive files. When a company or and individual clients or customers are still actively doing business with your company, the file is still active. If for more than five years no transactions have been made, it can be regarded as inactive.

Likewise, correspondence files like copies of incoming and outgoing letters, memos, reports with 5 years onward should be destroyed or placed in storage according to your preference.

For inactive files, it should be move to archives to avoid overcrowding of papers in the filling cabinet.

Class Activity

Assign the class to visit two or more different offices to find out the filing systems use by them. You can compare the filing system of a medical office or of the legal office or of a general corporate office.

Report this in class.

LEARNING ASSESSMENT   SCORE _____

NAME_____ YEAR/SECTION_____ DATE_____

I. Arrange the following according to group. 1. Arrange by unit the subjects/names to be filed; 2. Arrange the files into alphabetical order; 3. This exam is under time pressure (it depends on the teacher; 4. Get a separate sheet of paper.

1. De Guzman Tomas   MacGray, Pedrino
   De Leon Thomas   McGray, Pepito
   La Solidaridad   Cecile R. Dela Cruz

2. Caritas Health Shield of Malabon
   Caritas Health Shield of Manila, Philippines
   The Caritas Investment of the Philippines
   The Makati Investment

3. Block 2717 Genuine Glass Company
   35th of Events Management
   999 Sardines Limited

4. Ramon Magsaysay De Villa
   Ferdinand Navarro De Vega
   Father Martin
   Sister Rose

5. Philippine National Bank Sampaloc, Legarda
   Philippine Rural Bank Sampaloc, Legarda
   Central Office Sampaloc, Balik-Balik
   Central Book Store, Sampaloc, Philippines

6. The Beauty of the River Spa
   Wishing Well of the Ladies
   Genuine Paradise of the Angels
   The Beauty and the Beast Parlor

7. Fun in the Phils., Bohol
   Show the fun Corp. Phils. Cebu
   Everything Go Ltd., Phils.-Japan Corp.

MODULE 9

TRAVEL ARRANGEMENTS

An administrative assistant or an executive assistant is more likely to be tasked for travel arrangements by his superior.

Although you can choose from among the travel agencies on the internet, still it takes time to find the best prices and coordinate the places the executive may want to visit. Careful planning is needed to ensure a smooth and happy trip of the executive.

1. Know the exact location, the addresses of where to go. Is the executive travelling to several places? Are there available airports on the places he will go.
2. If the executive is attending a business meeting or a conference, consider the date of his arrival which is the day before the event to allow plenty of time for preparation. But of course, you have to ask if he prefers to get to the destination early or arrive last minute.
3. Booking should be at least a month in advance. Ask him if he wants to use his credit card airline rewards, or a specific airline. Ask if someone will pick him at the airport or he will need a rental car upon arrival.
4. If the executive need a hotel accommodation, booking should be two to three weeks before arrival. Ask what hotels does he enjoys staying at, or does he have credit card for specific hotel?
5. Make sure the executive have an up-dated travel documents, like a passport with at least six months validity period before the expiration date. A visa for entry into the country that

requires one. What airline mileage account his travel miles should be deposited into.
6. Confirm what he prefers to be seated: first class/business class. Understand the executive's seat preferences: aisle, window, or middle. Front of the plane or back of the plane. You can also ask about his meal preferences and book them accordingly.
7. Call the travel agency or do it by you and make the arrangements. Print the travel itinerary and carefully read it. Make sure those flights, hotels, car rentals show confirmation numbers.
8. Remind the executive to make sure that all necessary travel documents are with him before departure. Give him a list of what you have arranged for him.

The executive assistant may package the trip. Package the air flights, hotel, and car, if possible. Ask for a discount when trip amenities are packaged together instead of purchased separately.

In the event of an unexpected flight delay or missed connection, a smartphone app like Hotel Tonight can help assistants find last-minute lodging for much less money than they would normally pay. The boss won't be stuck in the airport or have to scramble to change the lodgings.

Create an Itinerary.

Since you already have all the information collected from making the plans, remember not to miss some data to include on the itinerary. This is a reminder especially when the executive is entering into his senior age. He will greatly appreciate if you can make his travel easy and comfortable.

If the executive will be visiting several cities and will have to hop from one airport to another, include in his itinerary the names of every airport that he will be flying from, the date and the gate number. Include the hotel contact numbers and the addresses of good restaurants near the place. Also, include the meetings and other events that he needs to attend.

Class Activities

If the students do not have any experience to travel in any other places aside from their hometown, it is a great idea if the teacher will arrange one for them. This should be coordinated with the head of the schools for their approval.

Guide your student in arranging the travel whether it is by land, water, or air.

LEARNING ASSESSMENT   SCORE _____

NAME_____YEAR/SECTION_____DATE_____

Q1. Explain how an assistant administrator could make a happy trip for the executive. 20 points.

MODULE 10

HANDLING MEETINGS

*Efficiency is a superficial quality.
It says nothing about whether you are effective.*

Companies have a calendar of conferences or events ahead of time while most of the organizations use meetings in the course of their work. The host should ensure that every member is aware of what they have to do before, during and after the meeting. It is also important to make sure that the organizing committees are completely informed of their roles since these meetings can be successful or unsuccessful, depending on whether they are managed properly.

There are several important principles to meeting management: determining situations that require a meeting, understanding types of meetings, planning a meeting, running a meeting, closing the meeting, and managing people after the meeting.

Situations Requiring a Meeting

1. When there is a new project. You need to meet with people who can help at the various stages of the project.
2. When there is a need to manage people. Managers need to meet with staff as a group or one-on-one to direct employees effectively.
3. Client meeting which may require to present product or service.
4. A meeting is an efficient tool to discuss issues or problems that concerns the organization and members.

Preparation

One of the responsibilities of an office manager, office assistant, secretary or receptionist is the ability to know how to prepare meetings. The report on what happens during the meeting and other various activities afterwards is a task that must be looked forward.

Types of Meeting

There is no reasons to call the meeting if it is not necessary. In calling the meeting an agenda is already prepared. People to attend to the said meeting are already informed one week before the said event. The meeting place is set with all the equipment to use and food to serve, if there is any. The time to spend should be considered since everyone has an important role to do in their own offices. People who are invited to attend will appreciate if there is already the set of time to start and to end promptly the said meetings. Lengthy meetings are really expensive on the part of the management and also to their units. It impedes the production of the company. The length and formality of a meeting will differ depending on what type of meeting it is. There are six basic types of meeting: monthly meeting, emergency meeting, presentation, conference, seminar and convention meeting.

1. **Monthly meeting**

A monthly meeting is a regularly scheduled meeting which was agreed by the management and the people who should attend at the scheduled date. This may be scheduled every first week or second week of the month, depending on what has been agreed upon. These meetings are recurring; they are easier to manage, with similar formats and agendas. Typically, these meetings are held on the same day and time, but they may be rescheduled if necessary. Usually an impromptu gathering happens on this type of meeting. Recording of meeting can be on electronic or taken by the rapporteur.

2. Emergency meeting

Is one that is called with very little advance notice. It is called to address a very serious problem that occurs inside the organization or outside the office. The discussion of this particular issue needs urgent attention on the part of the people concerned. The length of time and format are dependent on the topic to be addressed.

3. Presentation meeting

Presentation meeting is highly structured. The presenter may be from the company itself or an invited guest. It is a meeting when one or more guests speak, and a moderator usually an insider leads the meeting. The purpose of the presentation meetings is usually to inform, to orient or to give additional knowledge and skills on the participants.

4. Conference

This is a highly structured kind of meeting. Company conference is annually done in a conference room inside the company. It is usually a board of directors or of the stockholders meeting to discuss the status of the company. Generally speaking, the recording of minutes for the corporation is not different from the recording of minutes of the previously discussed type of meetings.

A teleconference is a telephone meeting of two or more locations through a telecommunications system. Telephone conferencing or audio conferencing are another terms of teleconference and is use when a team members are thousands of mile away.

Videoconferencing is a high-quality audio and video meeting among two or more people in separate places by means of computer networks.

5. **Seminar**

Is typically educational where someone with expertise provides participants with specific information. It may be held inside the company premises or most often outside the company, like hotels or on academic institutions.

6. **Convention.**

A convention meeting or formal assembly of members or delegates, representatives, or of a political party, fraternal society, profession, or industry. The participants are diverse and coming from different places. It is a practice or procedure widely observed in a group, especially to facilitate social interaction.

Conversely, presentations and seminars and conventions require a different seating arrangement where all participants can see the speaker, but do not need to see one another.

Planning a Meeting

To determine whether a meeting is necessary, consider the problem that needs to be solved or the issue that must be addressed. If all that is required is dissemination of information, then a memo or email may be sufficient. If you need information, decide if you can get that information from one person or if a meeting with several people is necessary.

Reserving the Meeting Room

For in-company meeting, the use of conference room are usually cleared through one person or department in charge of assigning the use of the room. Give the date and time of the meeting so that it will be reserved to you. If the meeting is to be held in a hotel or other places outside the company, arrangements must be made several months in advance. If it is a kind of convention, six months to a year is to be considered for the arrangements of the place. Reservation may include a number of people who will be spending several days at a hotel.

Always make sure that the space reserved for the meeting has adequate facilities, such as, adequate space, lighting and ventilation, comfortable chairs, tables, speakers table, lectern or podium and sound system.

Arrange for Outside Speaker

If someone from outside the company is to speak at the meeting, you will probably be asked to assist in making the arrangements. Since some speakers are booked for months in advance, you should contact him as early as possible. When you contact the speaker provide him the following details:

1. Date, time and location of the meeting;
2. General information about the organization;
3. Nature of the audience;
4. Purpose of the meeting;
5. Number of attendees;
6. Type of presentation the speaker would give;
7. The professional fee;
8. The expenses to be paid, such as hotel accommodation, meals, transportation, and others.
9. When the speaker has agreed to attend the meeting, ask for his resume to be used in introducing him.

Preparing Agenda

An agenda is a chart of procedures to be followed in conducting a meeting. The agenda should indicate the desired outcome of the meeting, the major topics to address, and the type of action needed. You may also want to list a name of a participant next to an agenda item. Below is a sample of procedures to follow in the agenda:

1. Reading of minutes
2. Treasurer's report
3. Committees' report
4. Unfinished business (matters to be continued should be itemized)
5. New business (list of matters to be considered)
6. Election and appointments of committees (can be omitted)
7. Adjournment

Send the notices to members and special guests.

Arrangement of materials and equipment

In planning for an in-house meeting, determine first how the meeting room should be set up. Check if any of the following are needed:

1. Notepaper or pencils
2. Badges for attendees identification
3. Bulletin boards, overhead projector, motion picture, tape recording
4. Glasses, water, beverages and food to serve
5. Telephone if necessary

Reporting on the meeting

The report of the procedures of a meeting is very important to the participants. The secretary may be assigned to take the notes. Taking the minutes of the meeting may be verbatim but in most meetings, only the significant facts and important action were taken. Motions, however, must always be reported verbatim. If in doubt on how much information should be included in the minutes, it is better to consult the manager before transcribing the minutes in their final form.

Facilitating in Meeting

When the meeting is underway, a meeting facilitator may need to establish some guidelines or rules for how the meeting should progress. Guidelines may include:

1. Attendees may give information or opinions after the speaker signaled that he is ready to accept opinions;
2. Participants should not interrupt when others are speaking;
3. One a participant seems to dominate the discussion, there is a need to ask the person to give others a chance to participate;
4. Be mindful of the time set in the meeting. If the time seems to be getting out of hand, announce to the participants to table a certain topic to be addressed at a later time, or ask for their suggestions for resolution so that they can move on to another topic.
5. In closing, read the summary of the minutes meeting, ask if there are issues not mentioned. The minutes should reflect all that has been transpired in the meeting.
6. In some type of meetings, an evaluation sheet is distributed to find if the meeting met the expectation of the attendees.

Follow Up Duties after the Meeting

After the meeting there are things to be checked especially it is an in-house meeting:

1. The room should be left in good order, like all equipment used are restored in their proper places;
2. Copies of the minutes of the meeting should be sent out the soonest possible;
3. Items that require future attention by your employer should be written on the calendar of the manager and of the secretary;
4. Make sure that all necessary forms are filled out by the participants who have incurred reimbursable expenses;
5. Letters of congratulations may be sent to newly elected officers;
6. Thank you letter should be send to speaker;

Class Activity

As a group, you may think of a topic that you would like to pursue for a one-day seminar.

Apply the knowledge you have learned in conducting a seminar.

To increase more of your knowledge and skills in conducting meeting, read the Parliamentary Procedures.

LEARNING ASSESSMENT   SCORE _____

NAME_____YEAR/SECTION_____DATE_____

I. Enumeration

A. Identify at least 4 problems in troubleshooting a meeting. Give a short note for each of the identified problems you may think.

B. What may be the problems in conducting a teleconferencing and video conferencing? Explain.

C. List down and explain the 6 types of meetings

MODULE 11

MANAGING FOR PERSONAL EFFECTIVENESS

Values are standard which one upholds as desirable traits and guide one way of life. Living with good values often gives the bearer a sense of control of his life because he knew what he wants and where to go. Working with values like having accountability and professionalism is important in one's career that enables a person to fit into his profession, colleagues, and superiors. Some individuals find satisfaction in their job because it matches their work-related values, while some end up hopping significant of them.

Consider the teachings in the bible, as you manage yourself for personal effectiveness.

"Look carefully then how you walk, not as unwise but as wise, making the best use of the time, because the days are evil. Therefore do not be foolish, but understand what the will of the Lord is." (Ephesians 5:15-17)

The foolish person misses the opportunities to make wise use of time, which causes him many problems. He doesn't know God's purposes for mankind. Hence, he also doesn't know what his purpose in life is.

"Make loving God and loving others a motivating factor in all you do, including work."

"In the same way, let your light shine before others, so that they may see your good works and give glory to your Father who is in heaven." (Matthew 5:16)

If all of God's creation will read and learn the word of God, he will open the doors of what you desire for life. Watch your attitude. For God knows the heart of men and he will direct you/us on every step as men walk on Him.

Work values

A person's beliefs about what is important or desirable to do which is related to his job are his work values. These core principles are an important part of who you are. It is important to know your own work values.

1. Determination

It allows you to focus only on achieving a specific goal without being distracted by less important things or spontaneous desires.

2. Self-confidence

Self-confidence can be developed by learning your capabilities. Have a positive attitude and believe that you can achieve the goals with sound mind and right heart. Self-confidence is manifested in speech, appearance, dressing, gait, and physical condition.

3. Persistence

It makes you keep moving forward regardless of emerging obstacles. There is a saying, 'the race goes not only to the swift but to those who keep running.' In addition, Powel, the former US Secretary of State said 'Success is the result of perfection, hard work, learning from failure, loyalty and persistence.'

4. Honesty and Integrity

It is the responsibility of each person to use their own individual sense of moral and ethical behavior when working with and serving others within the scope of their job. The aforesaid biblical verses can help you to be honest and to hold and maintain your integrity. It is declared in Proverbs 19:1 'Better is a poor person who walks in his integrity than one who is crooked in speech and is a fool.' In Proverbs 11:3 'The integrity of the upright guides them, but the crookedness of the treacherous destroys them.'

5. Self-Motivated

A self-motivated person requires very little direction and supervision. Grab the opportunity to learn new skills, methods and techniques. Take extra tasks and responsibilities without any prodding from others. Keep up with the current changes in your field of specialization.

6. Professionalism

Professionalism is someone who takes pride in their work, behavior and appearance. They maintain high-quality work and are detail oriented. They are enthusiastic about their work and optimistic about the organization.

7. Loyalty

According to 1 Corinthians 16:13-14 'Be watchful, stand firm in the faith, act like men, be strong. Let all that you do be done in love.'

Also in Proverbs 21:21, 'Whoever pursues righteousness and kindness will find life, righteousness, and honor.' What does this mean in terms of loyalty in today's workforce? It means love your work and honor the one who gives you bread for living.

How to become a Professional

"Would you tell me, please, which way I ought to go from here?"
"That depends a good deal on where you
want to get to," said the Cat.
"I don't much care where —" said Alice.
"Then it doesn't matter which way you go."

Where are you now on your career? As a student of Administrative Office Management, it is just right for you to make a plan of your future career. As a starter, many would start planning to get any kind of job. Maybe some will be given the opportunity to apply for a management position earlier than you thought. Wherever you are on your career ladder now or in the future, you should know how to plan your career.

A plan with explicit goals provides structure and focus for your learning ensuring you make the most of your learning opportunities.

Ask yourself these questions to help clarify your goals and begin planning.

What skills/knowledge do I have?
What role do I want to pursue?
What skills/knowledge do I need in my current/future role?
Where do I want to be in my profession five years from now?
What skills/knowledge will I need to be effective in that role?
How will I judge the quality of my work?
How does my practice impact on the school/community/office I serve?
Based on data, what do I know about my school/community/office's needs?
How do local, regional and national goals/initiatives impact upon my learning goals?
How can I improve or strengthen my practice?
How can I work with others to address my goals?
How will I know I have accomplished my learning goals?
Are my learning goals SMART – specific, measurable, achievable, realistic and timely?
How can I embed the professional development strategies I choose into my work day?
Do I wish to share/discuss part or all of my professional development plan with the person I report to?

Research indicates that working with others will enhance your learning and promote lasting improvement and change in your professional life and work environment. Also, focus on improving learning as the overall goal of professional development. A few of the many activities or strategies that you might consider are:

Get summer job to experience working in the corporate world;

Enroll on skills where you want to further develop: ex. Communication skills;

Keep up to date with new technology and learn to use it;

Find a mentor to help you in your career development;

Read daily newspaper, books on personality development, and other books of your interest;

When your plan is completed, take a step back and ask yourself the following questions:

Do the goals and the plan reflect your needs as well as those of your organization and community you will serve or about to serve?

Does your plan reflect new learning and growth, not just time and effort?

Are your goals clear?

Have you used data to determine your goals?

Do you include collaborative activities in your plan?

Does your plan include reflection on the outcomes of your plan?

Have you included methods of assessment?

Think strategically.

Think Like a Leader, most people want to take a more strategic approach to their work but are often unsure what that really means. Planning and executing is about how you do what needs to get done; strategy, is about asking what we should be doing.

A good professional development plan will be based on your understanding of where you are in your career cycle, what motivates and demotivates you, your values and your skills/competencies.

Characteristics of Successful People

Success is define differently by people. Some for having achieved financial security. Some for having good position in an organization; for a student having an academic excellence or being a leader. Others define success for having good name in the community that is recognized and respected. Despite these differing definitions of success, successful people themselves have similar characteristics.

1. Successful people have self-confident but not arrogant. These people are true to themselves, knowing their strengths and weaknesses, knowing their capabilities without forgetting the values and integrity to get their goals.
2. They are willing to grow by challenging their limits of knowledge and experience. They are open and appreciate feedback of what people think about them.
3. They reflect and learned through experience. They are self-critical by understanding what they have done and could have done better. They take pride of the good job they have done. Know that people who excel enjoy what they do and do what they enjoy.
4. Observe Others. Learn how others interact with people, observe who are effective and who doesn't. Learn their mistakes and guard yourself not to repeat that mistakes. Stay connected with people

"Fail to plan and you plan to fail".

Case Studies

Procrastination Problem

Mable is 43 years old. She married Biff 21 years ago. She says she is in a good marriage. They get along well. Mable and Biff have been Christians for 35 years. He is an executive for a local accounting firm.

Mable has been working as a trainer for an insurance company. Both Mable and Biff are successful, making over $250K per year collectively. They have been members of their church for 13 years and are active in various ministries.

But Mable says her devotional life has become dull and boring for the past few years. She describes herself as self-confident, persistent, hardworking, calm, serious, easy going, good natured, extrovert, enjoyable, and sensitive to the feelings of others.

For years Mable has struggled with procrastination. There are certain things she does with ease, and people consider her to be successful. But there are other things that Mable just can't seem to come to grips with as far as completing the tasks. She puts them off until the last minute and sometimes she will let them pile up, which creates tension in her soul and marriage.

Biff is not sure how to help her, so she comes to you.

Question

Where would you begin with Mable?
What questions would you have for Biff?
Why is she a success in certain areas of her life, but a "seeming failure" in other ways?
What do you think are the ruling motives of her heart?
What else do you want to know about her?

Stress Problem

Poppy Castle had a secure job and what she thought was a happy home life. Her husband then suddenly divorced her and moved to Australia, leaving Poppy with a young child and a house with a large mortgage.

First Reaction

"When John (my husband) left me with a child and the house to pay for, my first thought was to give up work. How could I cope with the Stress of childcare and all the household expenses by myself? I had a relatively secure job, and some good prospects, but the wage wasn't that great.

"My friends at work, though, told me to hang in there. They felt that because I was good at my work, I should stay put and apply for whatever help I could in the way of benefits, and so on.

"I took my friends' advice, but I began to feel stressed at both home and in the workplace. The financial pressure was getting me down.

"A chance for promotion then came up, so I applied for it. Everyone said I should get it, but because of the stress I was under, I didn't prepare properly. I also didn't pay enough attention to the questions at the interview. So, of course, I failed."

Threat of Redundancy

"Failure of this sort doesn't do your self-esteem any good. Still, I had to get on with things. My friends were a great help, and so was my manager. She told me that there'd be other chances for promotion and I'd get there in the end.

"Then another problem arose in the form of Redundancy. The redundancy was a rumor, but the company was going through a rough patch, and job losses were all that people could talk about.

This upset me, because despite the promotion knock-back, I was coming to terms with my life.

"The redundancy talk turned out to be just that - talk - but I could have done without the rumors. I knew all this stress was beginning to affect the quality of my work."

Workplace Stalker

"And then to add to my troubles, a guy called Peter from Accounts began harassing me. One day out of the blue in the canteen, he asked if he could sit next to me. He then said he wanted to go out with me.

"Another relationship was the last thing on my mind, and I explained this to Peter. But over the next few weeks, he phoned me, emailed me, and came to see me at my desk, trying to get me to go out with him.

"Frankly, the pressure of this on top of my financial worries, made me think seriously about leaving work. In fact, in a moment of panic and stress, I wrote a letter of resignation and gave it to my manager."

Turning Point

"This was something of a turning point. My manager advised me to take a day off and think carefully about what I was doing. She didn't want me to leave, and she knew that there was going to be another opportunity for promotion within the next few weeks.

"I said that was fine, but I was stressed about Peter. My manager listened to what I told her, and then said she'd see what she could do about him. What in fact she did do was see Peter's boss the next day. Between them, they banned him from seeing or communicating with me at work.

"After this chat, and once my manager had put Peter in his place, so to speak, things started to look up. The promotion opportunity did come again, and I did succeed the second time round. Things are still tough financially, but with the support of workplace friends and my manager, I'm much happier."

Meet Florian – Creative Thinking

Florian is an online marketing director for a startup based in Europe. He really loves what he does for a living which is staying on top of online marketing trends and chasing the next big thing on the web. Some people describe him as a workaholic as he is infamous for never skipping a day and working late.

Different people prefer different ways of working. A lot of people like working within a framework whereas others like to be more free when they try to get things done. The latter group of people are what some call "creative" types – people that find it very difficult to stay within the lines. Florian is someone who fits in this category and he finds it very difficult to stay within a framework. He is very good in thinking ten steps ahead, but has problems making the first five and following up from there.

Florian didn't come to us directly for help. It was one of his business partners, someone who is very Asian Efficient, who asked us to work with him to improve his personal and business productivity. Florian found it very difficult to pinpoint exactly what he needed to work on, so his business partner described to us what some of the obstacles were that needed to be addressed:

He has no organization system nor any task management system.

He is unreliable over email.

The are no productive habits or rituals in his life.

Knowing how to prioritize business objectives.

No separation of personal and work space.

Transitioning to a Mac setup.

Florian was aware of some of his leakages that prevented him from achieving peak performance:
An irregular sleeping schedule.
Going partying a lot and dealing with hangovers.
Working on low-value tasks he didn't want to deal with.

Leverage Points

For Florian to find his leverage points, he needed to focus on them properly. The energy and passion that Florian puts in his work is what helps him get a lot of things done, but it's the lack of priorities that makes him sometimes redirect that energy in the wrong direction. When you are always chasing the next big thing you tend to lose sight of what is most important right now.

What he lacked was the proper overall picture of what his high-value activities were and finding a way to delegate or outsource his low-value tasks. We recommended for him to work closely with his business partner to determine what the highest priorities are and then work on those one-by-one. A "silent cockpit", designated time for focused work, needed to be made a priority every single day at the same time. Since he is working in a fast pace and fast changing environment, he needed to sit down with his business partner twice a day to determine what the highest priorities were.

The next missing piece was introducing rituals, habits and systems in his life (more about that later). Without them it is very easy to get sidetracked and get disorganized. Whenever you see people that you describe as "chaotic", it is usually due to a lack of systems and routines in their lives. For people like Florian, the creative type, they naturally don't like to work within a framework and this was a major challenge for us.

While having no current systems in his life, having one or a couple is better than having nothing. We introduced a couple frameworks to him, but made them very simple and flexible. It was "just good enough" for him to work with them while at the same time giving him the freedom to do this work. We showed him how to setup his task management system (a very simplified GTD) and stressing the importance of separation of work space and personal space.

Leakages

Florian needed to address his bad habits:
Sleeping.
It turns out that Florian is nocturnal and prefers to work late in the hours and sleep during the day. We suggested to sleep and wake up around the same time every single day, as long as he aligns his working hours with his natural body rhythms.
Nights out.
Everyone needs to have a healthy balance of social energy. In order to prevent that from going out of hand, we recommended to go out no more than twice a week on fixed days and to drink a glass of water in between alcoholic drinks (if any) to prevent hangovers.
Delegation.
To prevent Florian from working on low-value tasks, we recommended to communicate more often with his business partner to determine what the highest priorities are and then to delegate the low-value tasks to someone else within the company. This would free up time for him to focus more on the more important things.

Rituals and Scheduling

With no rituals and routines in his life, this was the most eye-opening part of the consultation for Florian. We introduced our standard morning ritual to him that we have seen many people benefit from.

Drink water (500 mL) first thing in the morning when you wake up.
Have breakfast (preferably protein-rich).
Exercise.
Do visualization exercises.
Work on personal development.
Do one MIT (most important task)

Before he started to work, we endorsed to go over a mini ritual that will help him prioritize on what needs to get done:
Review long-term company goals.
Assign 3 tasks to do.
Note any low-value tasks that might be urgent and should be delegated.

His evening ritual:

Review the day.
Drink a glass of water.
Stretch.
Reading.
Go to sleep.

Efficiency System

The most important part of this consultation for Florian was to introduce systems and rituals into his life. Life can be very chaotic when there are none of them present.

Source: C. C. Lundberg and C. Enz, 1993, 'A framework for student case preparation', Case Research Journal, 13 (Summer), p. 144.

www.ingramcontent.com/pod-product-compliance
Lightning Source LLC
Chambersburg PA
CBHW030854180526
45163CB00004B/1564